Original title:
A Slice of Melon

Copyright © 2025 Creative Arts Management OÜ
All rights reserved.

Author: Gideon Barrett
ISBN HARDBACK: 978-1-80586-422-6
ISBN PAPERBACK: 978-1-80586-894-1

The Sweet Promise of Afternoon

Beneath the sun's warm glow, they lay,
Seeds of laughter tumble and sway.
Juicy dribbles down the chin,
A circus act of fruity sin.

With every bite, a grin escapes,
Summertime in funny shapes.
The sticky hands, a sticky fate,
Who knew snacks could celebrate?

Harvesting Joy from the Vine

In a patch where giggles bloom,
Tall tales of sweetness fill the room.
A fork in hand, a mission bold,
To taste the tales that summer told.

With each crunch, the laughter rises,
Nature's gifts in funny disguises.
Sticky cheeks and silly grins,
Who knew fruit could spark such wins?

Nature's Celestial Offering

Plucked from fields where jokes abound,
In every bite, pure joy is found.
The stars aligned for fruity cheer,
With every slice, we hold it dear.

As juice squirts and laughter flows,
A comedy show where nature grows.
With friends beside, the fun is loud,
In every slice, we're fruity proud!

The Rind's Embrace

Wrapped in the skin, a treasure hides,
Giggles leap like joyful rides.
With each squish, odd shapes arise,
Mirthful moments in disguise.

The rinds can laugh, the seeds can cheer,
A feast of humor draws us near.
Laughter sharp as a tangy zest,
In a goofy fruit game, we are blessed!

Lush Green Delights

In the fridge a treasure lies,
Bright and round, a perfect prize.
Jokes abound, oh what a fate,
Juicy giggles on my plate.

Each bite bursts with laughter's cheer,
Summertime's joy, oh so near.
Sticky fingers, sweet delight,
Under sun's warm, friendly light.

The Sunlit Heart

Round and happy, a sunny orb,
Full of sweetness, no need for a door.
I take a bite, and joy resumes,
Can't help but laugh, chaos looms!

Seeds pitch like tiny balls of fun,
Chasing friends, oh, we just run!
In every splash, a giggle springs,
Nature's gift in sunny flings.

Tasting the Vibrance of Summer

Bright like laughter, juicy and bold,
Nature's candy, we're never too old.
Friends gather 'round for a sweet retreat,
Sipping summer, can't be beat.

With each scoop, a smile we share,
Dripping juice, we haven't a care.
Laughter bounces, the moment's prime,
In this feast, we lose all time.

Harvest of Juicy Memories

Plucked from vines, sunlight beams,
Tales of flavor, sweeter than dreams.
Slurp and chuckle, we reach for more,
Joyful bites keep spirits soar.

In the garden, laughter flows,
With every crunch, our friendship grows.
Juiciness drips, we dance and play,
Summer's bounty on full display.

Summer's Serenade in Every Bite

Under the sun, the sweetness flows,
Juicy bursts like silly shows.
Laughter drips down every chin,
Delightful chaos, let the fun begin.

With seeds like confetti on the grass,
Each bite's a giggle, oh, what a pass!
A fruity prank in every slice,
Taste a joke that's oh so nice.

The Dance of Flavors in the Heat

Belly flops on a sunny day,
Tasting joy, come join the play.
The flavors twirl, a fruity spree,
Each nibble dances, wild and free.

Sweet nectar drizzles, slip and slide,
Refreshment bubbling like a tide.
With sticky hands and smiles wide,
A taste of summer we can't hide.

Fields of Refreshing Abundance

In patches bright, the colors tease,
Harvest fun with every squeeze.
Green hues burst with laughter's song,
Nature's pranks, they can't go wrong.

A splash of juice on funny hats,
Who knew snacks could be such chats?
Rolling on the grassy floor,
Every bite brings laughter more.

Vibrant Slices of Nature's Bounty

Between the laughter, colors blend,
Silly stories seem to transcend.
Chomping down, we're in a race,
Juicy smiles all over the place.

Bouncing bites, a funny treat,
Like tiny drummers, they'll take a seat.
With every munch, the giggles grow,
Summer's gift, come taste the glow.

The Secret of Sweetness.

In the fridge it hides, a green delight,
With a grin so wide, it's quite a sight.
When it's sliced, joy starts to reign,
Who knew bliss was found in grain?

Seeds lined up like tiny crews,
In my bowl, they play the blues.
Every bite a giggly dance,
Fruity fun, it's pure romance.

Juicy Whispers of Summer

Under sun's warm, teasing rays,
Fruit with laughter blooms and plays.
With a splash of juice, oh what a scene,
Bliss in the park, bright and green.

Children's giggles mix with the breeze,
Sticky fingers, and sweet expertise.
What a riot, this summer treat,
Juicy whispers, oh, what a feat!

Sweet Nectar on the Tongue

A burst of joy, a giggle burst,
In every bite, sweetened thirst.
It slips and slides, a playful thing,
No other snack makes taste buds sing.

Laughter bubbles on the grill,
As we munch, the world stands still.
Let's create a silly song,
For this fruity fun won't last long!

The Green Gold Beneath the Sun

Underneath the waving leaves,
A treasure waits, oh how it deceives.
Slice it open, the joy expands,
Gold on plates, the fruit demands.

Bouncing seeds like little toys,
Harvesting laughter, oh such joys.
Tiny bites make summer cheers,
Until it's gone, we hoot for years!

Nature's Green Elixir

In the garden, a fruit so round,
Juicy laughter can be found.
Sticky fingers, grins so wide,
Sweetness drips, like joy inside.

Nature's treat, a slice divine,
Each bite, a moment to unwind.
A slippery game, the seeds do flee,
Chase them down, just you and me.

Vibrance Among the Foliage

Under leaves so lush and bright,
Unexpected delight in sight.
Color pops, a jungle feast,
Every crunch, a playful beast.

Wild laughter dances in the air,
Fruits and giggles everywhere.
A feast where nature wears a grin,
With every slice, the joy begins.

Every Bite a Summer Memory

Sunkissed days and warm embrace,
A juicy trip to fruity space.
With each bite, the sunshine beams,
Every flavor bursts our dreams.

Friends gather in the sunny glow,
Funny faces as juice starts to flow.
Sloppy giggles, sticky hands,
In every bite, a world expands.

Echoes of the Sun's Kiss

Beaming bright, the golden hue,
Nature's laughter, oh so true.
Chewing joy, we sing a song,
With fruity vibes, we all belong.

A picnic spreads beneath the tree,
With raucous sounds of jubilee.
Who spilled juice? It's quite a mess,
But with each bite, we're feeling blessed.

Childhood Memories in Green

In the summer sun, we play,
Juicy bites that make us sway.
Laughter echoes, seeds we spit,
Messy faces, all a hit.

Grass stains meet the sticky skin,
The sweet delight, where fun begins.
Chasing dreams, just let them flow,
In this moment, we all glow.

Wearing smiles, not a care,
Racing friends, with bites to share.
Innocence wrapped in laughter loud,
Memories cherished, forever proud.

Associating Warmth with Flavor

Golden sunlight fills the day,
Flavor bursts in a playful way.
Sticky fingers, laughter shared,
Simple joys, none compared.

Picnic baskets, laid with flair,
All of us without a care.
Juicy treasures, bright and bold,
Stories of summer, we all told.

Every taste evokes a cheer,
Brings us back to laughter's ear.
Moments sipped like sweetened tea,
Warmth and joy, so carefree.

The Divine Essence of Sweetness

A juicy smile, sweet and round,
Children's giggles, all around.
The essence that makes us sing,
Happiness in a little ring.

In the shade, we make a mess,
Sticky crumbs, but who would guess?
Divine moments, flavors dance,
In each bite, a silly chance.

Sticky hands and sunny ways,
Laughter echoes, endless plays.
Melodies of sweetness fly,
Bringing joy, oh, my oh my!

Notes of Paradise in Each Bite

Taking bites, where flavors meet,
Every taste, a joyful treat.
Notes of paradise afloat,
In this bliss, we happily gloat.

Dreaming under the bright blue,
Moments sticky, all so true.
In the laughter, joy ignites,
Paradise in playful bites.

Twirling under skies so wide,
Nature's gift, we'll not abide.
Savoring each moment now,
To these memories, we'll forever vow.

Unveiling Nature's Treat

In the garden, a treasure waits,
Bright and round, it celebrates.
Slip of a knife, the juice flows free,
Laughing seeds dance in glee.

Fruits in hats, they're quite a sight,
Wobbling like they've taken flight.
With every bite, the giggles burst,
Refreshing fun, refreshing thirst.

Whispering Seeds of Delight

Hidden secrets within each slice,
Seeds like whispers, oh, so nice.
A fruity giggle, a squishy cheer,
Jokes on the table for all to hear.

Plopped on plates, a wild parade,
Sticky hands and juice cascade.
With every seed that makes a splash,
A laughter fountain, oh what a clash!

The Bursting Joy of July

Summer sun brings a juicy thrill,
Sunshine pockets, what a skill!
Lemonade's nice, but let's be bold,
Summer's laughter, a story told.

As we munch and sip, oh so sweet,
Sticky fingers, a funny feat.
Mom's in the kitchen, she starts to sing,
Puns and giggles, what joy they bring!

Crisp Reflections on a Hot Day

Beneath the sun, we take a seat,
Melons giggle, oh what a treat!
Chilly bites in the summer haze,
Joyful nights, and silly plays.

Each slice smiles with a cheeky grin,
Sunburned faces, where to begin?
Juice running down, a slippery race,
In the warmth, we find our place!

Juicy Sunshine on the Palette

In the garden, colors bright,
Fruits laughing in the light.
Wobble waddle, seeds in tow,
Summer's joy, a fun-filled show.

Splitting smiles with every bite,
Sipping sweetness feels so right.
Splashing juice with all my friends,
Laughter echoes, never ends.

Sticky fingers, can't resist,
One more taste, I know I'll miss.
Belly full, we roll around,
In fruit laughter, joy is found.

Refreshing Eden's Gift

Beneath the tree, we gather 'round,
A treasure chest of joy is found.
Color burst, a vibrant spree,
Nature's candy, wild and free.

Giggles bounce with every slice,
Underneath the sun, so nice.
Seeds like confetti on the ground,
In this feast, pure joy is found.

We dance with fruit, a silly show,
Bright delight with every flow.
A juicy giggle, oh so sweet,
Eden's gift, can't be beat!

Moonlit Dreams and Summer's Glow

Under stars, we share a treat,
Juicy laughter, oh so sweet.
Moonlit giggles fill the air,
In this moment, we don't care.

Serenade of fruit and fun,
Crisp delights beneath the sun.
Slurping sounds, we chuckle loud,
In the dark, we're feeling proud.

Spinning tales, the night so swell,
Every drop, a magic spell.
With fruity dreams that never end,
In our hearts, we all transcend.

The Dance of Sweet Juice

Dip and swirl, a juicy trance,
Pelting laughter in the dance.
Sipping nectar, what a treat,
Feet are tapping, oh so sweet!

Splashes bright in every flow,
Melody of joy, we glow.
Twisting flavors, sweet delight,
With every sip, we feel so light.

Fruits on sticks, our twirling fate,
Life's a party, we celebrate.
In the rhythm of the squeeze,
We find our joy, we find our ease.

Juicy Whispers of Summer

In the fridge, a treasure sits,
A bouncing ball of juicy bits.
We slice it up, oh what a treat,
Sweet juice dribbles down our feet.

Seeds like confetti, the fun won't cease,
Witty fights of melon fleece.
We laugh and munch, no time to spare,
Summer loves to play, we don't a care.

The Fruitful Serenade

Oh wobbling wonder of grassy shade,
In sunlit glows, our fun is made.
With juice that squirts and laughter loud,
We make a mess and feel so proud.

Rind helmets donned, we're ready to go,
In a fruit fight; it's all in the flow.
Each battle cry, a fruity jest,
In this sweet kingdom, we are blessed.

Sun-Kissed Delight

Chubby slices on a plate,
Each bite is like a sunny fate.
We giggle as we munch with glee,
Who knew a fruit could make us spree?

Laugh lines gather like tasty bites,
When fruity laughter ignites the nights.
So grab a fork, let the games begin,
In this fruit parade, we all win.

Sweet Nectar of Light

A splash of sunshine, juicy surprise,
With every nibble, sweet joy flies.
We toss the seeds like tiny dreams,
Creating chaos with our schemes.

Splashes of giggles, the world's delight,
As we dance in the sun's golden light.
This fruit of joy, no frowns allowed,
We're all just clowns, loving it loud.

Cravings of the Afternoon

When the sun is high and bright,
I wander in search of a juicy bite.
Laughter dances on the breeze,
I find my snack with such great ease.

A giggle hides in the sweet delight,
Sticky fingers, oh what a sight!
With each bite, I feel divine,
Juices drip as I sip my brine.

Friends gather round, grinning wide,
We toss the rinds, unashamed, side by side.
The world slows down, laughter spills,
In this moment, joy fulfills.

As the afternoon fades to dusk,
I treasure each bite, it's a must.
With every chuckle and every cheer,
I savor the fun of this time of year.

Harvested Dreams

Out in the fields where laughter grows,
I dreamed of treasures where the sunshine glows.
Plucking sweet wonders beneath the trees,
Each one a gift, my heart feels at ease.

Friends join in, a merry crew,
Competition brews with each bright hue.
Who can eat the most, we jest and tease,
Belly laughs follow like the buzzing bees.

Juicy tales of summer's past,
Moments like these, I wish to last.
Chasing memories like seeds that scatter,
In our hearts, the joy will matter.

As shadows stretch, we say goodbye,
With sticky hands and laughter high.
Though the sun will set, our joy won't cease,
In harvested dreams, we find our peace.

A Slice of Sunshine

Oh, the sun has finally spread,
Bright laughter dances, joy widespread.
With each cheerful squish, oh what a treat,
A golden glow beneath my feet.

Slicers ready, we gather around,
To see who can make the silliest sound.
With each bite, giggles ignite,
This fruity feast is pure delight.

The juice may drip on my chin so wide,
But I wear it proudly, it's my cute pride.
Friends tease me, and so I grin,
For in this mess, the fun begins.

As sunlight fades and dusk draws near,
We share our laughs, stories that cheer.
For in this moment, friendships shine bright,
In every sticky slice, there's pure delight.

Melodies of a Juicy Past

In the attic of memories we climb,
Echoes of laughter, a treasurable time.
Each juicy bite tells a story or two,
Moments of joy shared among me and you.

The rhythm of summer, we hum along,
As we munch our way through this fruity song.
Rinds and giggles scatter on the ground,
In this juicy symphony, happiness is found.

Grandma's tales of her youthful spree,
With cheeky grins and tipsy glee.
Biting down, the taste takes flight,
Memory sparks as flavors ignite.

As we gather now, a merry crowd,
Laughter echoes both clear and loud.
With each ripe slice, we toast the past,
In melodies sweet, our love will last.

The Garden's Fresco of Joy

In the garden, laughter lives,
Where every fruit does cartwheels,
Chasing bees in silly jigs,
Nature's dance is full of squeals.

Patchwork of colors on display,
A playful feast for all to see,
With giggles mingling with the spray,
As juicy treats burst forth with glee.

Frogs leap, wearing hats of green,
Bugs in ties, all dressed for fun,
In this patch, it's a funny scene,
The laughter's ripe, for everyone.

Gather 'round, the fun won't cease,
Savor bites that play and tease,
In every morsel, joy's release,
A garden where the heart's at ease.

Sunlight Trapped in Rind

Beneath the sun, a tale unfolds,
The sweetest secrets wrapped so tight,
In jackets red, orange, and gold,
Each bite reveals a burst of light.

With friends, we play the tasting game,
A slosh of juice—a cheeky splash,
Who knew a grin could taste the same?
As laughter spreads with every smash.

Syrupy giggles flow and gleam,
Like sticky fingers on our cheeks,
We dive into this sunny dream,
In flavor lanes where joy just peaks.

Hide the seeds, oh, what a jest,
The chomp and chew ignites a cheer,
Each moment savored is the best,
With sunlight trapped, we draw it near.

A Symphony of Sweetness

In the bowl, a riot grows,
Colors dance like they're on stage,
A medley made of nature's prose,
With a laughter that knows no age.

Spoonfuls jive, they jig and sway,
Each bite a note in perfect key,
Sticky sweetness leads the way,
To the tune of jubilee.

Flavors clash, yet harmonize,
As tongues play tricks, and laughter lifts,
Who knew the joy of tasty ties,
Is hidden in fruit's funny gifts?

In this concerto, we all delight,
With cheerful hearts, we sing along,
As nature's bounty feels just right,
A symphony of laughter strong.

Summer's Delectable Embrace

Summer wraps us in its arms,
With a fruity hug that's hard to miss,
In all the charm and taste it charms,
We squeeze and munch in pure bliss.

Picnics pop with playful bites,
In sun-kissed fields, we laugh and cheer,
Juicy stories take flight like kites,
Making memories bright and clear.

Rind hats perched on smiling heads,
Water fights break out with glee,
Melody of peace in spreads,
A feast of fun by the big oak tree.

As summer fades, we raise our cheers,
To sweet embraces, oh so fine,
In every morsel, joy appears,
A delicious dance, a tasty line.

Visions of Melon Fields

In sunlit realms where sweetness grows,
The fruit with stripes puts on a show.
With every bite, a splash of glee,
Like summer's laughter, wild and free.

A farmer's dance, a joyful sight,
With melons rolling left and right.
They tumble down the grassy hill,
Creating chaos, what a thrill!

A seed-spitting contest, oh what fun!
With every aim, we laugh and run.
The juicy drips, a sticky mess,
Who knew a treat could cause such stress?

In my dreams, I dream of greens,
Of striped delights and raucous scenes.
Where laughter reigns, and smiles abound,
In fields of fruit, pure joy is found.

A Splash of Sweetness

Oh, the orb so round and bright,
It brings my taste buds pure delight.
With laughter bursting at the seams,
It's like a party in my dreams.

I take a bite, the juice cascades,
A sugary river, a fun charade.
My shirt's now dotted, a fruity art,
But giggles are found, that's the best part!

Friends all gather for a feast,
With melon hats, we're quite a beast.
Who knew a fruit could inspire such cheer?
We laugh until we are in tears!

A slice of joy, so cool, so sweet,
This silly fruit can't be beat.
With every bite, a silly dance,
In the land of laughter, there's always a chance.

The Art of Juicy Indulgence

A noontime treat, a festive cheer,
The juicy fun draws all my peers.
With every slice, a giggle blooms,
In this fruity world, there's no room for gloom.

With sticky fingers and messy faces,
The joy of biting leads to races.
Oh look, there goes a slippery chunk,
And in this moment, we're all a bit punk!

A recipe for fun, the laughter swells,
With our fruity smiles, all is well.
The drips and spills, what a delight,
In the art of indulgence, we take flight.

Fling the rinds, let's make it rain!
With every round, we feel no pain.
Mirth and munching as good friends do,
In this juicy art, we find something new.

Refreshment from the Garden

In the garden green, the giggles rise,
With miracles grown beneath sunny skies.
The best of friends, we gather near,
For a feast of joy, and silly cheer.

A treasure hunt, oh how it's done,
With hidden fruits beneath the sun.
We dig and laugh in pure delight,
The juicy bounty, our appetite.

Every bite, a whispered song,
A melody of fun, nothing's wrong.
With every crunch, we spring in place,
Sharing smiles with sticky grace.

With golden sun and laughter loud,
The fruity feast, it makes us proud.
Refreshment blooms from root to sky,
In this merry garden, oh my, oh my!

The Harmony of Summer's Aroma

In the garden where giggles grow,
Laughter echoes among the rows.
Sweetness drips and spills like tea,
As sunbeams dance wild and free.

A fruit so grand, it wears a grin,
Its joyful scent brings out the skin.
With every bite, a splash of cheer,
Who knew fun could taste so clear?

The bees buzz loud, a comical show,
Chasing the sweetness, to and fro.
While birds squawk jokes from the trees,
Nature's punchline, if you please.

Underneath the wide sky's dome,
We munch our treasures, far from home.
The summer's aroma in a crazy whirl,
A fruity festival, let's give it a twirl!

Tangy Whispers of the Orchard

In the orchard where trees sway and bend,
A tangy treat is waiting, my friend.
With flavors bold, it starts to sing,
As the merry air gives each a fling.

The leaves rustle like laughing gobs,
As fruits collide with sunny blobs.
A peck here, a nibble there,
Each bite says, 'Life's best without a care!'

A juicy joke lands on my chin,
As I grin, it rolls back in.
The sweeter the taste, the louder the fun,
In this wacky orchard, we've barely begun!

Who knew fruit could tickle the tongue,
And make us sing as if we're young?
With every crunch, a giggle flows,
In tangy whispers, the laughter grows!

Taste of Eternal Summer

When warmth hits the tongue, it's a burst of delight,
A flavor that dances from morning to night.
With each juicy piece, the sun winks high,
Summer's promise, oh me, oh my!

Colors collide in the happiest way,
As playful bites brighten the day.
Smiles are served on each sunny slice,
Joy's recipe calls for a dash of nice.

With sticky fingers and laughter galore,
We dive right into this fruity folklore.
A memory made with each playful chew,
Eternal summer, we mean it, it's true!

So grab a spoon and take a leap,
Into flavor's pool, the fun is deep.
With a taste that tickles and warms like the sun,
This summer feast, oh what a run!

The Vibrant Pulse of Nature

In nature's heart, where vibrant things glow,
The pulse of fun makes our faces aglow.
With colors bright that dance and leap,
Tasty treasures make us giggle and peep.

Giant green orbs, a wild menagerie,
A circus of flavors, come take a glee!
Each bite a burst, a crisp delight,
Nature's comedy, a pure appetite!

The sun's a clown, the clouds a jest,
As I crack and munch, feeling so blessed.
With silly faces, the harvest arrives,
A banquet of giggles, oh how it thrives!

So join the fest, let laughter ensue,
Nature's vibrant paint, a wondrous view.
With each tasty scoop, we leap and cheer,
For life's delicious, and summer's so clear!

Thirsty Hues on the Tongue

In summer's heat, a juicy delight,
A burst of colors, oh what a sight!
Giggles arise with each juicy bite,
Sweetness drips down, oh what a night!

Children squeal, they race and they chase,
Trying to lick it, it's a funny race!
Sticky fingers, smiles on each face,
Nature's candy, a sweet embrace!

Vibrant Joys

A vibrant splash on the picnic scene,
Juicy laughter where kids convene!
Faces covered in sugary dreams,
Who knew life's best joy could be so green?

With every wedge, an uproar grows,
Tickling tastes beneath summer's blows.
Shouts of joy where the laughter flows,
Oh what a treat, everyone knows!

Sunkissed

Under the sun, sweetness galore,
Bright and cheery, never a bore!
Sunny laughter from shore to shore,
Each slice brings comedy, who could ask for more?

We giggle and munch with sticky smiles,
Contentment found in juicy piles.
Skipping around, we've no denial,
Sunkissed delight stretches for miles!

The Dance of Sweetness

Every bite a dance, look how they twirl,
Colors of joy, watch them unfurl!
Juicy battles in their funny swirl,
Nature's treasure, a fruity pearl!

Giggling friends in a watermelon fight,
Chasing laughter under the bright light.
With sweetness dripping, it feels so right,
What a delight, what a pure sight!

A Symphony of Colors

A tune of flavors, converse and bind,
Juicy notes, hilarious and kind!
Nature's palette, oh what a find,
Each slice a joke, perfectly timed!

Under the sky, in carefree delight,
With every crunch, we giggle with might.
The symphony plays, laughter takes flight,
Colors unite in a joyful sight!

Where Sweetness Meets Nostalgia

Juicy memories drip with glee,
Childhood laughs are wild and free.
In the summer sun we danced and played,
A sticky treat that never stayed.

Every bite's a giggle fit,
Wobbly dribbles, oh what a hit!
With every taste, a story told,
Of sticky hands and hearts of gold.

The flavors burst, a pop of cheer,
As laughter echoes, crystal clear.
A past so sweet, it makes me grin,
With every slice, the joy begins.

Oh, to relive those sunny days,
In the fruit's warm, vibrant rays.
Each refreshing bite brings back,
A time when life was on the right track.

The Freshness of Lush Lands

In vibrant fields, we roam and run,
The fruit of laughter, oh what fun!
Crunchy bites in the summer heat,
A playful taste, so light and sweet.

Plump, green globes like bouncing balls,
Nature's way of breaking falls.
With every crunch, a giggle rolls,
As nature's bounty fills our souls.

On picnic blankets, smiles collide,
With juicy treasures, we take pride.
In every slice, a zany dream,
The fruit that sparks our wildest schemes.

So let's embrace those sunny days,
In orchards where the laughter stays.
With every munch, a memory made,
In the lush lands where joy won't fade.

Nature's Liquid Sunshine

Like raindrops kissed by warming rays,
A burst of joy in sunlit ways.
Dripping colors, sweet and bright,
A liquid laugh that feels so right.

With every chuckle, bright and loud,
A fruity hug, we feel so proud.
Nature's nectar, so divine,
Life's little jests in every line.

In pools of laughter, we all dive,
Each juicy bite keeps dreams alive.
Golden drops that make us grin,
The sunshine wrapped in fruity skin.

So grab a slice and join the cheer,
For liquid sunshine, ever near.
In bites of bliss, we find our fun,
A delightful race 'til day is done.

Color and Flavor Intertwined

With vibrant hues, the fruits collide,
A carnival where flavors ride.
Sweet and tangy, round and bright,
A tasty race that takes to flight.

In glistening bowls, they dance and sway,
Colorful rivals in a playful fray.
Sipping joy from every piece,
Laughing heartily, never cease.

Wobbling slices make us cheer,
A fruit fiesta, full of cheer.
Taste explosions, what a sight,
In every bite, pure sheer delight.

So let the colors burst and blend,
A fruity fun that has no end.
As laughter mingles with each bite,
In a vibrant world that feels so right.

Emerald Reflections

In the garden, green and bright,
I found a fruit, a pure delight.
Juicy chunks, a feast to share,
Seeds everywhere, a fruity dare.

Bite one, two, what a mess!
Dripping juice, I must confess.
Laughter bubbles, one big grin,
In this fun game, I can't help win.

Friends gather, laughter rings,
Count the seeds, what joy it brings.
A juicy challenge, oh what fun,
Under the sun, we've just begun.

Each bite brings a playful jest,
Sticky fingers, but we're blessed.
With every slice, a giggle grows,
Our happy hearts in sweet repose.

Laughter in Each Bite

A fruity ball of sunshine bright,
Tasting this gives pure delight.
Giggles echo with every chew,
Juicy drips, oh what a view!

Who knew snacks could spark such glee?
Barefoot games, just you and me.
Seedy smiles and cheerful chimes,
Creating festive, silly rhymes.

Hands sticky, but who cares?
We laugh aloud, forgetting stares.
Packed with joy, each slice, a thrill,
The best memories, they always fill.

So here we munch, what a blast,
Honor each sweet slice amassed.
With every giggle, we ignite,
The joy we find in each bite.

The Essence of Refreshment

Summer days swelter and burn,
But oh, sweet joy, it's our turn!
Chopping chunks, the laughter flies,
A waterfall from our prize.

Fuzzy skins and shades of green,
Dancing juice, a perfect scene.
With each splash and juicy grin,
Life's a party, let's begin!

All around, the laughter swells,
With every bite, the story tells.
Coolness wrapped in smiles so wide,
A fruity joy we can't hide.

So slice away, let fun unfold,
With flavors bright and stories told.
Embrace the humor, seize the day,
In every bite, joy finds a way.

Glistening Dewdrops

Morning dew on a summer morn,
Bouncing juice, laughter reborn.
Bubbles pop, a playful fight,
Each juicy drop a pure delight.

Chomping down, our faces gleam,
In this world, we plot and scheme.
Tickling taste buds, oh what fun,
Sticky fingers, we've just begun!

Friends all gather, sharing wide,
With every slice, we throw aside.
Messy faces, let's not fret,
In this moment, you won't forget.

Glistening joy, like morning light,
In every bite, we take to flight.
Let's dance and laugh, come join the spree,
A fruity fun-filled jubilee!

The Sweetness of Innocence

A green orb sits upon the stand,
With seeds like tiny specks in sand.
Children giggle, fingers stick,
Juicy treasures, quick to lick.

Sliced and served on a picnic plate,
Wobbly giggles come from fate.
A splash of juice upon the nose,
Sticky laughter, who really knows?

Bright red smiles come shining through,
Reminding us of skies so blue.
Innocent bites, we munch and cheer,
Skipping shadows, free of fear.

So here we munch with glee and grace,
As nature's candy brings a face.
Laughter echoes, joy in sight,
Sweet slices make the world feel right.

Threads of Sunlight and Juices

Golden rays fall on the ground,
A little fruit rolls round and round.
Sunbeam kisses, dew drops cling,
Nature's joy makes our hearts sing.

Each slice glistens, a shiny show,
A dance of colors, a vibrant glow.
We take a bite; the world's on pause,
Juicy droplets get applause.

Funny faces, a juice-filled mess,
The kitchen's chaos becomes a fest.
We sip and slurp, it's all a game,
This juicy chaos never feels the same.

Threads of sunlight weave through yells,
And fruity laughs spill joyful bells.
With every bite, sweet laughter rings,
In this fruity world, we spread our wings.

The Colorful Symphony of the Garden

An emerald hue in the summer's breeze,
A sweet delight grows from the trees.
Each pluck reveals a candy flair,
Laughter dances in the air.

Colors with giggles met our sight,
Like rainbow tapestries of delight.
Pink and green on a wooden plate,
Where laughter seems to congregate.

Tiny fingers reach and grasp,
Juicy bites that make us gasp.
Songs of crunch and squishy bliss,
In every nibble, a sugar kiss.

In gardens rich with sounds so bright,
We love the mess, it feels so right.
A symphony of juice and cheer,
Let's crunch and munch the summer near!

Nature's Sunlit Delight

Under the sun, what do we find?
A little green orb, truly kind.
With a grin that could charm the day,
It's nature's treat, hip-hip-hooray!

We cut and slice with giggles loud,
Juicy splatters, we feel so proud.
Under trees, we sit and feast,
Feeling blessed, we're nature's beasts.

Cucumbers watch with envy wide,
As we delight in our juicy pride.
Sticky hands, and laughter shared,
It's the perfect snack, so well-prepared.

Nature's joy in every bite,
These flavors bring pure delight.
We savor each drop, a sweet parade,
In sunlit glories, memories made.

Celestial Refreshment

In the sky, a snack so bright,
With a hue that's pure delight.
Floating high, it brings a cheer,
A heavenly munch without a fear.

Plucked from clouds, it tastes like fun,
Sweet as laughter, second to none.
Sipping stars infused with glee,
What a feast for you and me!

Nibble on this cosmic treat,
Juicy bits that can't be beat.
Giggles burst from every slice,
Who knew heaven had such spice?

With each bite, a giggle rolls,
Tickling the most serious souls.
A fruity joy, so absurdly grand,
Let's have a banquet, hand in hand.

Luscious Melodies

A tune so sweet, it fills the air,
With flavors bright beyond compare.
Every nibble, a note so clear,
Dancing on tongues, oh what a cheer!

In a bowl of laughter, we all dive,
Taste buds waltzing, feeling alive.
With each crunch, a chorus sings,
The joy of fruit, oh how it clings!

Tropics whisper in every bite,
Joyful rhapsodies take flight.
Silly flavors swirl around,
As giggles spark, sweet and profound.

Harvested from a giggling grove,
Tickling troubles, making us clove.
A melody of tastes, so refined,
Finding bliss, and joy intertwined.

Juicy Daydreams

In a world where drips don't stain,
Dreams are fruity, free from pain.
With each bite, whims come alive,
Rolling flavors that happily thrive.

Bouncing juices, laughter flows,
Colors dance and chase our woes.
Crisp and vibrant, giggles gleam,
Swirling in a summer dream.

Dripping smiles, a playful mess,
This fruity feast leads to happiness.
Scooping up joy with a spoon,
Sunshine dances, and so does the moon.

Clouds reshape into a cool treat,
Every bite makes life complete.
Dreams become the sweetest thing,
Juicy wishes that laughter brings.

Woven with Sunshine

Sunbeams stitched into every slice,
Nature's craft that's oh so nice.
Golden threads of laughter spun,
Brightened faces, joy begun.

Woven tightly, a tapestry sweet,
With each piece, life feels complete.
Chasing worries into the past,
This delightful bite holds fast.

Colors burst like fireworks bright,
Every chew a spark of light.
Giggles twirl with each juicy taste,
Moments savored, never a waste.

Nature's blanket of bright delight,
Wrapping us in warmth so bright.
A fruity hug for all to share,
In this joy, we love to dare.

Fountain of Sweetness

In summer's sun, they gleam so bright,
A bowl of joy, what a delight!
With dribbles down my chin, oh dear,
I laugh at how I shed a tear.

The seeds like treasures, hidden small,
I spit them out, a fruity ball.
Giggles echo, as I compete,
To launch these seeds - it's quite a feat!

The juice cascades, so rich and bold,
In sticky hands, it's pure gold.
My friends all join, a tasty race,
To see who can win this juicy chase!

With every bite, a burst of cheer,
The sweetest fun we hold so near.
We share the laughter, shade, and zest,
A fruity feast, we're truly blessed!

The Essence of Warm Days

In twilight hours, we gather round,
With bowls of bliss, the joy abound.
The sun goes down, but smiles stay bright,
As we devour this tasty bite.

A sticky prize, they slip and slide,
With playful hands, we can't abide.
The seeds like missiles, sent on cue,
We laugh and shout, 'I got you!'

Between the slices, flavors burst,
A summer party, quenching thirst.
The noise of munching fills the air,
With each sweet slice, we're free from care.

So gather round and take a seat,
With laughter shared, it can't be beat.
These golden hours, where joy combines,
Are truly ours, like fruity vines!

Where Flavor Meets Joy

A picnic spread beneath the trees,
With cheeky bites, a summer breeze.
As laughter flows with every slice,
The taste of joy is oh so nice!

The juice it drips, a colors bright,
As friends all cheer, 'This is just right!'
We toss our seeds like little planes,
The silly aims bring all the gains!

They giggle, chomp, and steal a bite,
Each moment savored, pure delight.
With watermelon smiles that say,
"We're living large, come laugh and play!"

The essence of fun, on sunny days,
Where flavor meets joy, in quirky ways.
Each bite a spark, a silly jest,
This fruity feast, we love the best!

Nature's Delicate Treasure

A patch of green, where laughter swells,
With treasures ripe, the sweetness sells.
I pluck a slice, and take a bite,
The taste of sunshine fuels delight.

As juice cascades, I'm caught off guard,
With sticky fingers, it hits hard.
My friends all laugh, they hold their gut,
A juicy mess, the funniest cut!

We trade our secrets, slice for slice,
This fruity bounty feels so nice.
With shouts of glee, we seek the core,
In nature's bounty, we explore!

So join the fun, and take a stand,
To celebrate with fruity hand.
Each chuckle shared, a moment measured,
In every bite, a bonus treasure!

Childhood Laughter and Juicy Savor

In summer's heat, we ran around,
With sticky hands and laughter sound.
The fruit so sweet, we'd bite and chew,
Our faces grinning, dripping too.

Playing tag in fields of green,
A fruity feast, like we were dream.
We shared our spoils with giggles bright,
Juicy tales under sunlight.

Sun-drenched Bliss

A picnic spread on grassy hills,
Chasing butterflies, catching thrills.
The sun above, a giant ball,
We munched away without a stall.

With every bite, a squirt of cheer,
We'd laugh and shout, no trace of fear.
Sandy toes and watermelon laughs,
Those sunny days, our happy paths.

Dreaming in Green and Gold

In dreams of green, the shadows dance,
With golden fruit, we take a chance.
Each juicy slice is full of fun,
Foregoing chairs, we sprawled and spun.

The summer breeze would play its tunes,
As we chomped bites beneath the moons.
Giggles burst like seeds in air,
A world of sweetness everywhere.

A Canvas of Flavors

On the canvas of our summer days,
The colors splash in juicy ways.
Twists of laughter fill the air,
As we paint memories everywhere.

A brave young painter, color bold,
In every slice, a story told.
We'd scoop up smiles, blend them right,
With laughter echoing, pure delight.

Summer's Savor

On a hot day, a juicy delight,
The seeds are scattered, oh what a sight.
I fumble and slip, it's quite a show,
Laughter erupts as the juice starts to flow.

In the picnic basket, it's king of the feast,
All struggle to grab, but I'm in the least.
With sticky fingers, we share a wide grin,
The sticky dilemma, where do I begin?

Under the sun, we take a big bite,
Faces all glisten, such a silly sight.
Who needs ice cream with laughter galore,
This summer treasure, who could ask for more?

As we nibble, the day slips away,
The fruit-filled giggles remind us to play.
With seeds on our shirts and smiles everywhere,
This laughter-filled moment, too perfect to bear.

Sun-Kissed Dreams in Each Bite

Bright and vibrant, a color so bold,
A snack so sweet, my heart it does hold.
I take a huge bite, juice splashes around,
Everyone's laughing, a mess that we've found.

The sun is blazing, it adds to the fun,
Each wedge I devour, oh, aren't we all one?
But wait, there's a seed, right here in my grin,
How could something so sweet cause such a din?

We play catch with the seeds, all in pure jest,
While our favorite snack puts our patience to test.
Slipping and sliding, oh, what a delight,
With sticky hands waving, we dance in the light.

At day's end, the shadows start to grow,
Our tummies are full, but our spirits still glow.
With chocolate smeared faces and hearts ever bright,
In the memory of summer, we'll hold this bite tight.

The Refreshing Heart of Nature

In the garden of laughter, a treasure bestowed,
A comedy show, by nature's own road.
Just one little slice, and chaos begins,
As juice drips down and we tumble in spins.

A nibble reveals, oh, such juicy bliss,
Yet somehow I'm caught in a fruit-flavored kiss!
My friends all erupt; they can't help but chuckle,
As I clean off my shirt, oh the fruity muckle!

With cheeks like pumpkins, we rival the sun,
You take one slice, and then we are done.
A battle of seeds, we laugh and we play,
Who'll make the longest? It's the silliest fray.

As twilight approaches, the fun's not yet done,
We recount our blunders; oh, wasn't it fun?
With nature's sweet gift shared amongst all,
The laughter of summer, the best kind of call.

Melodic Bites of Sunshine

A dance of delight on the table it waits,
The golden sphere beckons, oh how it elates!
With a slice through the flesh, it sings out so bright,
Each nibble a note in the warm summer night.

As I raise up my piece, it slips from my hand,
Down it goes rolling, oh, isn't it grand?
We chase after joy like the fruit on the floor,
A slapstick parade, who could ask for more?

So simple, so sweet, the laughter we share,
With friends all around, it's a fruity affair.
Juice-stained and giggling, we tumble and slide,
Each moment together, we're filled up with pride.

As the day starts to fade and the stars take a peek,
Our hearts are so full, there's no way we'll squeak.
In the melody of summer, so playful and light,
In each juicy moment, we find pure delight.

Nature's Sunlit Treasure

In the garden, colors so bright,
Lush delights dance in the light.
Round and plump, a cheeky treat,
Nature's candy, oh so sweet!

Buzzing bees with a jolly hum,
Plotting mischief, here they come!
Sipping nectar, feeling grand,
Nature's bounty, oh so spanned!

Squishy joys and sticky smiles,
Riding laughter for a while.
Seeds like gems in a playful fight,
Spitting stories, what a sight!

From picnic baskets, giggles flow,
As each bite leads to more show.
Fruitful chaos, pure delight,
In this garden, hearts take flight!

Floating in Honeyed Air

In the kitchen, scents entwine,
Sticky drips, our arms align.
With each slice, a happy cheer,
Spoons get messy, friends appear!

Sunshine smiles on weathered chairs,
Lemonade within our swears.
Forks are dancing, sweet and bold,
Stories shared, as dreams unfold.

Laughter bubbles, sweet surprise,
Flying forks and playful eyes.
Mouths agape in gleeful trance,
Who knew fruit could lead to dance!

Clouds of sweetness fill the day,
As we munch our cares away.
A slice here, a bite to spare,
Joyful chaos fills the air!

The Verdant Feast

Under leaves, a table set,
Gather 'round with no regret.
Colorful smiles, vibrant fun,
All join in, the feast begun!

Fruits like orbs of giggly dreams,
Bursting with flavor, oh it seems.
Jests and jabs from cheeky friends,
Laughter echoes, never ends.

Sticky fingers, lost in bliss,
"Who took mine?" we giggle, this!
Nature's bounty in our hands,
Creating joy across the lands.

With our plates piled high with cheer,
Sharing bites, we hold them dear.
Each forkful brings a silly tease,
A verdant feast, oh please, oh please!

Juicy Echoes in the Breeze

With each munch, a squishy sound,
Joyful echoes all around.
Spitting seeds like little darts,
A silly game that warms our hearts!

Blowing bubbles, fruity cheer,
With every bite, we shift gear.
Little drips and wild grins,
The fun begins as friendship spins.

Laughter rolling through the grass,
Each bite brings a pop—what sass!
Furry friends join in the mess,
Chasing crumbs, we love this fest.

Daylight fades, but fun stays near,
With juicy echoes, hearts sincere.
We thank the sun for every bite,
In breezy tales of pure delight!

Cradled in Green

In the garden, big and round,
Laughter echoes, joy is found.
Wobbling shapes that tease our sights,
With every bite, the fun ignites.

Slick and shiny, bright as day,
Sneaky critters want to play.
With sticky hands, we take our chance,
In this fruity, silly dance.

Seeds sprinkled like confetti bright,
Spitting them with all our might.
Giggles burst like summer rain,
Who knew snacks could bring such gain?

Craving flavors, sweet and bold,
Stories shared, forever told.
With every munch, the fun multiplies,
Oh sweeter than the sunlit skies!

The Essence of Softness

What a treat, it's soft and sweet,
A fuzzy gift, just made to eat.
Juices dripping, colors glow,
With every bite, a burst, a show.

Fruits collide in a juicy swirl,
Creating chaos, watch it whirl!
Sticky fingers, laughter loud,
In this feast, we feel so proud.

The subtle giggles, the playful fun,
Every slice, a race to run.
Popping seeds like tiny peas,
In this madness, joy's the key!

With every nibble, smiles spread wide,
Celebrating nature's pride.
So much laughter on our quest,
Who knew such snacks could bring such zest?

A Tongue's Delight

Oh, such joy, a treat divine,
A slip and slide, a taste so fine.
Colors dance, laughter flows,
In this sunshine, sweetness glows.

Crunchy bites and squishy plays,
Sticky cheeks in sunny rays.
Every flavor, a wild cheer,
A party here, from far and near.

Sipping juices, a splashy game,
Seeking snacks, we're all the same.
Yummy treasure, nature's gift,
With each delight, our spirits lift!

Joyful munching, let's embrace,
A gathering, a happy space.
Every nibble, laughter's sound,
In fruity bliss, we are unbound!

Generations of Taste

Grandma's recipe, oh so sweet,
Sandwiches that no one can beat.
Licking fingers, tales unfold,
In every bite, memories bold.

Whispers soft of days gone by,
Underneath the clear blue sky.
Kids and critters chasing round,
Chasing sweetness that we found.

Jumping splashes, summer fun,
Sunsets glimmer, day is done.
Taste traditions passed along,
In this rhythm, we belong.

The laughter echoes, hearts unite,
Every flavor, pure delight.
Generations sharing cheer,
In our hearts, they linger near!

www.ingramcontent.com/pod-product-compliance
Lightning Source LLC
Chambersburg PA
CBHW070006300426
43661CB00141B/260